OF ARCHITECTURE

OF

The Territories of a Mind

ARCHITECTURE

VLADIMIR AZAROV

Illustrations by Nina Bunjevac

With an Introduction by
Edward Kay

Library and Archives Canada Cataloguing in Publication

Azarov, Vladimir, 1935-, author
Of architecture : the territories of a mind / Vladmir Azarov ;
illustrations by Nina Bunjevac ; with an introduction by Edward Kay.

Poems.
Issued in print and electronic formats.
ISBN 978-1-55096-559-9 (paperback).--ISBN 978-1-55096-574-2 (epub).--
ISBN 978-1-55096-577-3 (mobi).--ISBN 978-1-55096-578-0 (pdf)

I. Bunjevac, Nina, illustrator II. Title.

PS8601.Z37O32 2016   C811'.6   C2015-906963-7
                                                      C2015-906964-5

Published by Exile Editions Ltd ~ www.ExileEditions.com
144483 Southgate Road 14 – GD, Holstein, Ontario, N0G 2A0
Printed and Bound in Canada in 2015, by Marquis Books

We gratefully acknowledge the Canada Council for the Arts, the Government of Canada
through the Canada Book Fund (CBF), the Ontario Arts Council, and the Ontario
Media Development Corporation, for their support toward our publishing activities.

Canadian Sales: The Canadian Manda Group, 165 Dufferin Street,
Toronto ON M6K 3H6 www.mandagroup.com 416 516 0911

North American and International Distribution, and U.S. Sales:
Independent Publishers Group, 814 North Franklin Street,
Chicago IL 60610 www.ipgbook.com toll free: 1 800 888 4741

contents

THE TERRITORIES OF A MIND

An Introduction by Edward Kay

The landscape of Vladimir Azarov's newest collection of poetry, *Of Architecture: The Territories of a Mind*, is surprisingly lively, given that it is populated by historical icons.

But these "territories" are no excavation of cultural ossuaries. A profound point becomes apparent as one explores Azarov's juxtaposition of lovely bones: his is a classically trained mind, just entered its eighth decade of life, still vibrantly trying to come to terms with that which we all ultimately face, the terrifying awareness of our own inescapable date with the black void of non-existence.

Azarov grew up in the Stalinist-era Soviet Union, where loss of self, both metaphorically and literally, was the occupational hazard of anyone trying to get ahead in life while avoiding all attention: it was a society in which the secret police kept their eyes peeled.

This is pointedly true in Azarov's case. He grew up in Kazakhstan, where his father had been banished along with his family to "internal exile" after falling out of favour with fellow members of the Communist Party. Later, the apparatchiks deemed even Kazakhstan to be too close to Moscow, and then imprisoned his father in a Gulag after a neighbour snitched on him for the crime of listening to a Voice of America radio broadcast.

The Soviet disregard for individual self-determination is in some ways a parallel to the ultimate lack of self-determination imposed on all of us by biology and an indifferent universe. So it's not surprising that the ephemeral nature of even the limited freedoms available in the Soviet Union, as well as the reactionary nature of the Communist leadership to culture, deeply influenced Azarov's outlook.

Azarov is an architect by profession, and this too informs his poetry. It is an inescapable truth, especially in an Old World context, that for an architect to make room to create something new, it is often necessary to destroy the work of an earlier architect. The uneasy combination of ancestor worship and parricide inherent in such a profession surely shapes Azarov's poetic view. Only the most-loved or most-immovable buildings survive such a process, and even the ones not pulled down by human will are eventually lost to erosion and gravity.

This sense of impending death, and certain if slow destruction, pervades this collection. It is present whether in an event as cataclysmic as 9/11, or an occurrence as casually horrifying as the notion of seeing your younger face staring back at you from a bathroom mirror.

And hence those references to the long-dead figures whose relevance to Western culture has been tested by time and has achieved permanence by popular consensus over generations, providing an intellectual and emotional pole star to give a sense of hope and meaning to the fading of the light.

That said, Azarov is at his best and most poignant when his poems draw from his own experience, the architecture of the territories of his mind. In such moments he makes his strongest emotional connection to the reader. There is little doubt what's on his mind, nor of the universal truth behind it when he writes of:

> *"... pre-historic fossils*
> *caught between layers of coal*
> *the seizure*
> *of a butterfly in flight*
> *an absent-minded insect*
> *accompanied*
> *by a stegosaurus in dense blind foliage*
> *outside the presumptions of poetry*
> *reality is real prose*
> *washing, after a run of waves,*
> *all prints away*
> *sorrowful footprints embedded in*
> *someone's solitary*
> *heart."*

He who thinks greatly must err greatly.
　　　　—MARTIN HEIDEGGER, "The Thinker as Poet"

I love not man the less, but Nature more.
　　　　　　　—LORD BYRON

KING LUDWIG OF BAVARIA

I

OF MADNESS

1

swans the colour of snow-pearl
circle the indoor pond
on the upper floor
of the Residenz Palace in Munich,
their lean necks
looping in obeisance at midnight
before the King's little punt
as it noses through dark waters
to an embankment where lackeys
in royal livery hurry past a bamboo
fisherman's hut to help him step out to join his tethered
falcons and peacocks on a carpeted slope
under an echoing arched ceiling
and an artificial illuminated rainbow
(he calls himself the Moon King)
entering a grotto –
his secret kingdom –
to a violin's mournful tune
and the water's babbling –
the two in morbid harmony

2

   out of his closet
of arcane memorabilia
he comes disclosing his fractured inner self

   isolated
he comes a soul whose
servants cannot ease his acedia

he comes to engage his restless fantasies
he comes on the spoor of his treasures
he comes to be among his beefy Rubenesque
                                        demi-gods

under azure-blue skies
flying figures lit up by flaring torches,
                        susceptible to music's ministrations
to the disputation between Van Dyck and Jordaens

all this helps him to forget his aloneness
as he surveys an old Flemish
                        landscape of
cold silver water

walls roofed by red riffled tiles
brick chimneys smoking
the wings of mills wheeling against
a pale sky confluent with the far horizon –
all reflected in a river along with

                                    a man
                        a boy
                                    a horse
                        a dog
                                    a herd of black
spotted cows, a green meadow
                        heavy with dew

3

the King feels a clamminess on the breeze –
                    squinting
he examines various canvases
then wipes away a spot of candle grease from and old oil
                    sprackled by time
dabs a handkerchief to his eye –

kindly servants offer him
a crystal glass
                    he sips
a little wine   sighing
taut, highly strung, he sleeps
watchfully, his blood starts,
forcing awake his high-voltage yodelling mind

the King's brain sparks bio-signals
                    he swans forward,
has shocking fantasies –
of how he might commit murder and how
to sit down and die –
how to forget the royal court's routine
Europe's bloody wars
the burghers' taxes   the peasants' taxes

"Ludwig II," said Richard Wagner "is so soulful and lovely, that his life must melt away in this vulgar world..." The young, handsome Bavarian King Ludwig was truly besotted with Wagner's music and wanted to become his patron. He offered to take all the financial burden away from Wagner leaving him free to create his art in an ideal atmosphere. To this end, King Ludwig installed Wagner in a beautiful villa close to the royal castle of Hohenschwangau.

5

obviously wistful, sudden vigour transforms into
images of architecture –
Herrenchiemsee –
Baroque and Rococo –
a sparkling ornamental blast –
                              fanciful, intricate, a sanctuary:
morbid and mutinous by temper he has had
his refuge built
by a thousand peasant artisans
as a scenic dream,
green woods wedged between white-capped Alps
sculpted castle towers
a nest of palaces
erected to rescue him from
meddlesome demons

6

the King absent-mindedly strolls
down long mirrored rows
                            of hollowed out rooms
                                    led on by
haunting soprano sirens in full flight
the Valkyris
of the Nordic Sagas
join him
so pale, so dignified
in his dreams,
led by Lohengrin –
by the King of the Nibelungs.

7

the Swan King smiles, enraptured by echoes that
resound through the lime trees
and above his castle towers
crenellated walls that reverberate around
his royal aloneness
reading Schiller aloud
to the cows
flaunting his aesthete's soul

At this time, Wagner's happiness was further enhanced by a meeting with a lady who was to become the third and last great love of his life. Ludwig requested the presence of the conductor and piano virtuoso Hans von Bülow and his wife Cosima. When Cosima and Wagner fell in love, Hans was prepared to sacrifice his unhappy marriage to the greater glory of Wagner's music.

9

who, wearing blue and white swan feathers,
strangled his doctor
and sat down in the dark lake
waters at Schloss Berg on Starnbergersee
to drown himself at dusk, saying,
"Eternity and infinity, I am in eternity and infinity."

II

OF MEMORY

Memory of sun seeps from the heart.
What is it? – Dark?

—ANNA AKHMATOVA

The wind herding white cumulus clouds

Condensing
Not into coming rain
But into trembling silhouettes
Around a land of
Gesticulating ghosts.
Almost transparent as they turn into a crowd
Not huge but all too real
Of faces that I remember.
With pounding heart I am aware of
The presence of their absence,
Bliss of airy footprints, unreal
Crowd smirking, gossiping, laughing,
O yes! they come to me
Like this young woman
Dalila? Why does she sing? Not talk?
Behind her a muscled, mischievous boy
Who must, it seems, share his every anecdote.
His laughter still infects me
As he asks, Are you actually in hockey's
Cradle? Canada?
I remember snow, hockey sticks, a puck,
Your stutter – stride,
Drunk, tipsy,

Decades ago.
Your only joy was hockey,
A bright blond girl cries
As she models in her mind a caricature

And I cry out to her! I don't look anything like that!
Then a discreet well-to-do young
Lady gets all my attention *hi hi* and I hear

What is Hecuba to him? Or he to Hecuba?

As an actor interrupts
Hamlet's monologue,
While a curly black-haired guy hurries up to me
Tuning his guitar to Pushkin's elegiac couplets,
Singing to Akhmatova's oseless slut

"Who ever said that one was born just once?" says Jacques Derrida in Presence and Absence. *"As I gaze out into the world I can say the world is present to my observing eye. Presence is, therefore, the main predicate for a text's meaning (its sense or its reference), despite the fact that this meaning is always absent and in need of reconstruction through reading or interpretation. In this way gaps, absences and deficiencies of all imaginable kinds are subordinate to a principle of presence."*

A modest smiling fellow pressing in on me,
So close my breathing has become his breathing!
Who's he? So familiar! His guilty smile
My younger face in the morning's mirror!
I AM YOU!
A silence hangs   no words   the crowd thins
All disappear
All melt into the air   all withdraw
The elegant girl waves her pale hand
Ghostly silhouettes wheel
Across icescape
Ascending to the white sky's absence,
Counter to gravity, counter to memory

"If the present moment can be repeated (i.e. remembered) then, preceding the present moment, is the possibility of its being repeated in memory (i.e., memory itself as repeatability). So memory precedes and exceeds the present moment, which we will have remembered. Memory, as tradition makes quite clear, ends up associated with death and the memorializing of the dead, or mourning, in a way that takes us back, always and from the beginning, to the second moment's absence."

SIGMUND FREUD

III

OF MIND

1

our mind rocks in a cradle inside
                              a round skull
a box a drawer
this naked breakable
                              bone cranium
the impact of completed thought

this shell encases
the inwit of our industry
the ground zero of our thinking,
                              our silver-grey cerebrum

of many
membranes
a vascular
interconnection

a cerebrum responsible for our
conscious though divided

hemispheres, left and right

that house living functions
such as speech
        the recognition of objects
and memory, and etc.
thalamus and hypothalamus
the geometric centre of this spatial entity
that regulates
        hunger thirst
sleep body-temperature divination
water balance blood pressure...

2

a bio-electronic
                     turned-on electric
                              substance
unceasingly accumulates
our thoughts
and stores them at the ready

                     thinking matter
phosphoresces
radiating sparks
pulsing trembling breathing
                     beating striking chiming
lying sitting eating drinking
multi-functioning while acutely conscious
of what is good
to exercise
                   to jog jump to leap spin
to dance waltz
a sensual material that needs
rest
sleeping yawning awakening
making new business

                    talking crying whispering
laughing trolling
reciting
          serenades
          subconsciously making love
and consciously
giving birth to a small spinning
                    sphere

3

"How does the physical brain rise to the psychological mind? How many Kings command that brain?"

"In Descartes' dualism, all phenomena is explained in terms of two distinct and irreducible principles, mind and matter, their only connection being the intervention of God."

"The mind is like an iceberg, it floats with one-seventh of its bulk hidden below water."

—Sigmund Freud

4

an iceberg
                drowning
in the deep dark recesses of a saturated
                    subconscious

the iceberg as lighthouse

as if lit from within an underwater station
                    the one-seventh of its bulk a myth
                        invented
byAlbert Einstein
          plus presumptive Freud's
                '10 percent myth'
                i.e. just 10% of our iceberg brain
is ever used!
          and why?
so that we might survive
our own probes and proclivities
and because of our fallow bio-God

as it turns out
we are not only limited in our ability to think as a form
of play but have

forgotten our

                    ancient abilities that were once
there with the roaring stegosaurus
facing
our own rock drawings

but then the thinking world got more
                complex
not just seeking bee smell as bees do,
no! no! no! but using all our
supply of brain cells
skeptical   critical
crying out, Now!

that was the '30s myth
                back in the time of Einstein/Freud
our modern
minds are
                verging
                on the edge of more and more incredible
                potential untapped
                information streams

of course, it's true
many neurons are

unnecessary
but in some cases,
an iceberg's deep bottom line
is ripe and ready

                    to serve any abstract
irrational or rational command
instinctive or intuitive intimate
intonation
poetic ravings or
rhythmical rhyming
lines   ornate stanzas   ghazals
                  or just plain narrative
                      but no matter the way

it is a stream
of energetic consciousness
that is on the march
sustained by a semi-hidden
subconscious
life
using 100% of our
                  iceberg's hemispheres

IV

OF ARCHITECTURE

1

architecture's future lies in two bricks,
as Mies said,
pre-historical survivors lie in the depths
of drawings on cave rock
walls, a fine art, surviving murals –
burning torches hollow
wavering fumes the warmth of flames
the cave's skinny bodies
their grasp in the bright blinding air
hunting to survive
the sun shines and then the rain pours
the trees' foliage is their roof
as foul weather forces them down on all fours
our ancestors fold their helpless
hairy hands over their heads
to make an umbrella
the streaming water courses
to their elbows, to the
grassy land
nature's architecture prior to two bricks!
And upright survivors

subsist under the
leaves' construction and – still – with no
sweat, no blood from hard-working builders

2

"A hundred times have I thought New York is a catastrophe and fifty times: It is a beautiful catastrophe."
—Le Corbusier

"Space and light and order. Those are the things that men need just as much as they need bread or a place to sleep."
—Le Corbusier

"The architect represents neither a Dionysian nor an Apollonian condition: here it is the mighty act of will, the will which moves mountains, the intoxication of the strong will, which demands artistic expression. The most powerful men have always inspired architects: the architect has always been influenced by power."
—Friedrich Nietzsche

"Less is more."
—Mies van der Rohe

"Less is a bore."
—Robert Ventury

"All fine architectural values are human values, else not valuable."

—*Frank Lloyd Wright*

"Architecture is 'frozen music'... Really there is something in this; the tone of mind produced by architecture approaches the effect of music."

—*Johann Wolfgang von Goethe*

"The physician can bury his mistakes, but the architect can only advise his clients to plant vines."

—*Frank Lloyd Wright*

"Here, then, is what I wanted to tell you of my architecture. I created it with courage and idealism, but also with an awareness of the fact that what is important is life, friends, and attempted to make this unjust world a better place in which to live."

—*Oscar Niemeyer*

"Architecture starts when you carefully put two bricks together. There it begins. *(As Ludwig Mies van der Rohe had been given "virtually a free hand to create the Toronto-Dominion Centre," the complex, as a whole and in its details, is a classic example of his unique take on the*

International style, and represents the evolution of Mies'
North American period, which began with his 1957
Seagram Building in New York City.)

Architecture is the will of an epoch translated into space."

—*Mies Van Der Rohe*

3

turning to history – turning to the careful
brickwork of walls
put up to withstand
the wind-driven cold – walls sustaining roofs
against rain snow
or the shocking sun's rays
beneath
an innocent pre-historic sky
above those sinful warrior epochs when
enemies and neighbours
gradually erected roofs over roofs
conquering the world with
zigzagging silhouettes,
architecture's handwriting
set against snow ice and rain

4

time however flies and weary slaves
hunker down under the sun's heat
hauling giant stone blocks past a
Sphinx's smirk to the giant triangle
the heavy oversized
and over-silhouetted pyramids with their
convoluted labyrinthine interiors
relentless time flies
inviting breathtaking lines of weightless
souls to strive
to reach to settle among beings beyond high heaven
to touch God's Gothic verticals
this brave crusade's materialistic quest –
two chiselled bricks or stones are the start of the search
for the divine poetic golden
architectural fleece

5

various constructions run up
the big blue sky fed by a bloody
crucifixion, cruising among
historical barbarians their excitement fighting with
stone heads wood and iron crosses loping on ahead
killing swords unsheathed
armour-clad horses galloping
out beyond civilization
cries and fits of the Inquisition's victims – the
tortured witches' salt tears that
freeze into ice beads of refined stone
architectural details
Gothic's lines of
splayed groaning martyrs
within arched spaces –
mourning bells dissolving
the suspense echoing sadly in the pouring
rain from the tongues of
sculpted gargoyle chimeras
sad afterword and wound of each Christian crusade

6

a devil's tail descends out of ideology
quintessence of fighting
saint of nothingness
lands lost among dense jungles of
glossy noble stones
arced materialistically
God's spiritual existence
which enslaved workers
created out of their sweat and blood –
a columned garden, a walled joy
to the eyes –
vistas from heaven's height
bird's eye view of holy art
of many styled architecture!
transparent marble leaves
intricately lighted sculpture
cement bushes on
granite soil, a complex geometry

7

artificially dressed nature in
clothes built out of rows of poetic serenades
caged birds eating golden grain having laid
ancient Greco-Roman gold eggs
in bloom beneath a gloomy
sky, cataclysmic catastrophes

8

two bricks are the beginning of architecture
two gothic Goliaths two twins
two tall handsome brothers
stand on tiptoe smiling
sophisticated spirits aloft in
mature long and lean bodies
stylish touch of metropolitan art, land
and sky, moving clouds, and also
angelic saviours who spin a new world's waltz
around the earth's night
and so do not pay attention to thieving devils,
those horned devils about to destroy all beings
pretending to be innocent insects in flight
dark ill-natured birds inside holy space
vengeful

9

two woe-struck gored Goliaths, on razor-sharp horns,
their armour
clattering in the air
transforming into a black hole
ground zero, a huge void,
steam covering all traces
of history, its empty foolish wars,
its dark revolutionary upheavals beheaded,
the whole planet's focused on architecture
two bricks two stones two columns
the placing of a beam or architrave, this is architecture,
a stable internal cosmic structure – having
from the beginning a cemetery of
destroyed memorials, monuments,
Pompeii's black ash shrouding the world souls
from Khufu's geometric giants
to the Acropolis, to the architecture
of the eternal in a city, Rome.

HOMER

V

OF WORDS

When words are scarce they are seldom spent in vain.
—WILLIAM SHAKESPEARE

1

From GORGIAS *by Plato –*

SOCRATES: Suppose that a person asks me about some of the arts which I was mentioning just now; he might say, "Socrates, what is arithmetic?" and I should reply to him, as you replied to me, that arithmetic is one of those arts which take effect through words. And then he would proceed to ask: "Words about what?" and I should reply, Words about odd and even numbers, and how many there are of each. And if he asked again, "What is the art of calculation?" I should say, That also is one of the arts which is concerned wholly with words... and suppose, again, I were to say that astronomy is only words – he would ask, "Words about what, Socrates?" and I should answer, That astronomy tells us about the motions of the stars and sun and moon, and their relative swiftness.

GORGIAS: You would be quite right, Socrates.

SOCRATES: Words which do what? I should ask. To what class of things do the words which rhetoric uses relate?...

2

Words words words – what's the matter
So many words? cheerful
Dionysian words – *crowd   mob*
Eating   imbibing   ingesting
Appollinian words – for heroes or
Intergalactic heroes – stalwart warriors or
Provocative thinkers
All are spoken written words
Passionate strict or serenic
Flying from mouths

Meaningful or meaningless
Words are signs or signals alerting
Each and every Pavlovian dog
The oratorical howl of that oratorical organ, the brain oracular –

3

Meaning within meanings
Graphic silver behind the glass
Abstract scrawls of convoluted scribbles
Phenomena devoid of intention   vectors
And ink   photographic verbs
To rhyme Petrarchan sonnets for Laura
To make a poor sinner's confession
To write an uber-hero's speech
To mitigate whining pleas made for the whole
World collapsed downloaded into a saga
Told in alliterative verse
To fire up lightning in a prophet's words
To inscribe the words *mob   crowd*
Knights   Kings – for readers   listeners

As the Devil urges a man into hell
With seemingly simple words
Birds in flight – such tempting
Waves riding on the backs
Of other waves,

A surge...

4

Newborn babies
At first! – this cacophony in our ears
A whorl of words – a knock on the
Membrane's door – or, explosion
On the tip of the tongue

An inner constructive meaning given
To the concrete world
Of a million billion trillion pages collected
The cosmic memorabilia of man's mind

5

The poet says:

"Like a poet, man lives"

Ambivalent between stones underfoot and
The stars, touching down on the land oh so ten-
tatively
For a time

Where he walks in the winter
And in the spring, stone-picks among
The crocuses

And then
Wanders through the world
With little or no awareness
Of his brief existence
Unembarrassed,

Yet creates poetry,
Sonorous songs on his
Pélerinage – a man
Himself made in his own image,
Art
Stalking amidst the
Beasts eating grass at the river's edge

Always armed by a new
Technology
Prepared to kill catastrophically.

6

Free by night and day
Man avoids the Acropolis, the
Sheltering stone temples

He listens not to the flirtatious

Caryatids' inviting Ionic voice

Nor does he lean against Doric
Poseidon's burly legs

The film The Ister *(2004) travels upstream along the historical river Danube toward its source exploring a number of themes, including: time, poetry, technology, war, myth, National socialism, the Holocaust, the ancient Greek polis, the 1999 NATO bombing of Yugoslavia, the voice-over, Martin Heidegger reading Holderlin's hymn.*

From the hymn poem "The Ister," by Friedrich Hölderlin

> *"... This one, however, is named the Ister,*
> *Beautiful he dwells. The foliage of the columns burns*

And stirs. Wild they stand
Erect among one another; above

A second measure, from rocks
The roof juts out. Thus it surprises
Me not, that he
Invited Hercules as guest,
Gleaming from afar, down there by Olympus,
When he in search of shade
From the sultry Isthmus came... "

In 1942, at the University of Freiburg, Martin Heidegger delivered a lecture course on the hymn poem "The Ister" (The Danube) by the German poet, Friedrich Hölderlin. Heidegger attempted to explore the meaning of poetry, the nature of technology, the relationship between ancient Greece and modern Germany, the essence of politics and human habitation.

7

Motivated by the Muse
Man purports to sail under the flag of Ulysses

Down the Danube or the Volga
Buffeted by the warm Black or
Ice-cold White seas singing the song
Of the Golden Fleece

And ends up dry-docked,
Using his sail for a tent, fleeced

8

Demi-gods,
Those young muscled bodies become
Wise old flabby men wearing philosophical togas

Who dive ethereally to the watery deeps or
Fly into astrological spheres or take off
On an instant technological run

Fire is with us.
Eager to witness the day's end

Blue flame of the blind poet, his
Blessed evaluation, line by line, of life –
It's time to put an end to games of cat-and-mouse
And open ourselves up to fragrant firs

To roam the crooked nighttime streets –
A man, open-hearted and free,
Turns his life into verse,
An heir to the ancient hexameters, pentameters

Philosopher and magic stone
On the edge of an abyss

"Like a poet, man lives"
in suspense

sailing lifelong on the earth

9

after Friedrich Hölderlin

I was a boy in a country of atheists
    their pagan gods, our God
    were peripheral,
        ephemeral

no one could protect me
    from the curses and cruelty,
    the fists of my school mates
        I played among trees and flowers

trusting their kindness, or behind
    closed doors where I drew up a future
    where houses grew by storeys
        like mushrooms, as tall

as skyscrapers in the movies
    where a boy could eat
    ice cream alongside girls
        where fields were without end

and emerald forests embraced
   ripening fields of wheat
   in black white movie reels
    grain, gold as a

summer's rain was warm and
   caressed my beamish face,
   a rumbling thunderstorm part
    of the jazz drumming

on the Voice of America
   which was banned and drowned out
   by an electro-hissing noise –
    that was a long time ago

I did not know the words, the name
   of the poet who would speak of woe, to me
   to all who were caught behind the lines of
    WWII – he lived a long time ago

and was German like our Catherine
   the Great – words so close
   to me when I was a boy
    and to me now also close:

trees were my teachers
melodious trees
I learned to love
among flowers
I grew up in the arms of gods

KAZIMIR MALEVICH

VI

OF GEOMETRY

Nobody untrained in geometry may enter my home.

—PLATO

(a first square)

the geometric inquiring spiral
leads to a cosmic height in art beneath
                the trembling restless ceiling of
being and time's reality

exploring and absorbing
              all palpable
              all objective
        visual subjects
then this inquiry wanders afield
outside an obviously inscrutable existence
to solve the convoluted formulas
of abstract non-objective subjects

an epistemology that is
              the comprehension
of life as art
as the geometric surgeon of inquiry's
poetic method
Kazimir Malevich

(a second square)

a Russian artist who plunges
behind Being's mirror
to seize innovation

in the laconic spirit
of an iconic Slav

birth

of the main math micro molecule

or quark
of the two dimensional
all lines and all surfaces
a many coloured
SQUARE

zero form graphics against words

a simple song
sonnet of living poetry
sounding much earlier than any philosophy
or prehistoric rock drawing

the transcendental Square is presented by

an artist on the coming
revolutionary

storm's eve

        dangerous times for humankind
given an inhuman
march
against the vulnerable images of ART

Kasimir Malevich's "Suprematism":

"Under Suprematism I understand the supremacy of pure feeling in creative art. To the Suprematist the visual phenomena of the objective world are, in themselves, meaningless; the significant thing is feeling, as such, quite apart from the environment in which it is called forth. Academic naturalism, the naturalism of the Impressionists, Cezanneism, Cubism, etc., all these, in a way, are nothing more than dialectic methods which, as such, in no sense determine the true value of an art work. An objective representation, having objectivity as its aim, is something which, as such, has nothing to do with art..."

"Under Suprematism I understand the supremacy of pure feeling in creative art."

(a third square)

idealistic hope for an ideal future
a quick breaking up of all illusions
creativity's evolved into Dante's

dark inferno
where a new crux for the avant-garde is forgotten

a premature newborn dead at its
birth after a bloody Caesarean section
the post-coup's Red Rough Repression
of Kazimir Malevich

alien change
becomes accusatory material leading toward
conviction – Geometric Art
                as hostile anti-Soviet
propaganda
                on the heels of
                        his successful Berlin exhibitions
        his lectures
for Bauhaus' Gropius
                his Klee Kandinsky close confluence

his life with Futurism
Cubism
Suprematism

(*the last square*)

however years went by and time's
                    spiral
Kazimir Malevich's trajectory
arcs ahead
    . to the incarnation
                of future human dreams
the vibrant contour of the
Square
            an artist's presence
                in the world

Scan the QR for Vladimir Azarov's conceptual video "Black Square"
which features *King of Geometry*, as read by Barry Callaghan.

Or view at: www.tinyurl.com/Azarov-BlackSquarePoem

VII

OF THE QUEEN
OF ENLIGHTENMENT

Yet this Tsar wasn't a man, or a Romanov, or even a Russian.
—JAY WINIK, *The Great Upheaval*

*Peter the Great was Tsar from 1682 to 1725. He opened Russia
to the West by building St. Petersburg out of the swamps found
along the banks of the Neva. The city was officially renamed
Petrograd, 1914-1924, and then Leningrad, and then St.
Petersburg again in 1989, after* perestroika *and the hauling
down of the Berlin Wall. The Winter Palace, erected between
1754 and 1762, was stormed in 1917, signalling the October
Revolution.*

1

A moonless winter night,
Moscow,
1744.
The sun had seemed, at dusk,
To drop out of the sky, leaving behind a lingering fog,
Like lagoon gas from Tsar Peter
The Great's day   six-
Foot-eight if he was an inch   who
Oversaw several thousand pile-
Driving serfs who were sucked under water
By the currents of the swirling White Sea,
Their bones a bed for
Ice palaces, canals, onion domes.

2

Well, yes! Here in this morning gloom
It is Moscow, but not Moscow winter
Weather: not sunny not frost-bitten   crisp
But gloom-struck and fog-
Bound. The Prussian Princess
Sophie and her Swedish mother
Are here to meet
A prospective groom   the Grand Duke
Charles-Peter.

On this glum Moscow morning she
Calls for a grey horse,
A stallion, and her travelling case of books.

3

The rows of palace rooms are lighted
By a run of crystal chandeliers
That illumine the spindle-
Thin Sophiechen.
The mirrors   parquet floors
Reflect her bejewelled dress.
"How do you do, my Figchen?"
A boy's voice behind her. She is
In fright—no ceremony about his appearance:
And leashed to him is a large hairy rat
The scared girl almost faints:
"How do you do, Grand Duke Peter?"

4

The mother bows and stands aside.
The boy smiles and says:
"I don't remember you as a girl.
But then, I don't remember being a child at all.
I'm told I was such a strange little boy but now
I am sixteen –
Ready to marry."
She: "Happy Birthday my cousin!"
He: "May I introduce to you a general
From my army of lead soldiers?"
The smart rat looks at her
Again Sophie almost faints.
"Don't worry he is polite
I have for you a secret –"

5

"Give me your ear."
He whispers: "I am in love."
(She thinks: "How fast he moves!")
He cries: "I am in love!
But she doesn't want to be an empress!
That nasty Russian girl!"
Sophie smiles very nervously:
"Really?"
He: "And my auntie sent her
Mother to Siberia."
(Sophie's mind: "So many
Secrets in the court!")
The rat yaps out loud
And yanks at the leash.

6

A sunbeam splits open the room
And the boy Peter goes away.
The German Princess starts her new life,
Now named Catherine
As is the Russian Orthodox convention.
And Peter also is converted from
Swedish Lutheran into
The Russian communion
Losing his other name, Charles.
What will happen later?
Sophiechen practices speaking in Russian.
Her head is dizzy and her delight
Changes shape every few minutes.
Each vowel tastes of a different colour.

7

Russia is beautiful. Summer
Comes. The nights are warm and
Pale, just the right light for walking in the park.
After dark, Catherine reads her books by candle flame.
Half-German Peter doesn't help her
To adapt. He anoints her, names her "Colonel,"
In his toy lead army. The sniffling
Floor rat is an appointed officer, too,
And Peter's three pet dwarfs, each called Colette, who line
Up the soldiers in the morning, also wear epaulettes.
Oh! The times! He's seventeen!
The Empress aunt in her gilt carriage
Is glad to proclaim:
"The Grand Duke is ripe
For marriage!"

8

*The Russian Enlightenment of the 18th century was pro-
foundly influenced by the French, especially during the first
part of Catherine the Great's reign. Famous for her cordial
relations with Voltaire and Diderot, she founded the
Hermitage Museum, the Free Economic Society, and the
Imperial Public Library – three pioneering institutions
aimed at the spread of education in Russia. Foreign intellec-
tuals – Diderot, Leonhard Euler, Peter Simon Pallas,
Giacomo Casanova, Alessandro Cagliostro – flocked to her
court. A Legislative Commission, convened at her suggestion
in 1767, brought out the Instruction, some 400 articles
copied verbatim from the works of Montesquieu. On the
advice of her learned correspondents, Catherine introduced
dozens of reforms and generally speaking, became the
model for who and what a benevolent dictator would be.*

9

The years pass in a partial haze of vodka.
The chary old rat yields his marital position to
His cheeky
Young son who is even
More hairy. Catherine is still
Colonel. Her marriage to
The weak-headed teenager looms as a huge
Miscarriage. To his rat friend,
He adds yapping lap-dogs and a squealing violin,
His latest passion.

10

Catherine closes her ears, buried in her books,
Or grips the neck of a horse galloping
Through forest distances to meet her
Friends Potemkin and Orlov.

11

Count Potemkin was a lover and adviser to the Empress, Catherine the Great. Though acutely aware of all the ideas loose in revolutionary France, she was out of touch with the condition of the millions of serfs in bondage in Russia. To sustain her sense of opulent well-being, security and isolation, Potemkin erected "cardboard" villages to line Catherine's route on her grand expedition down the Dnieper to visit the Crimea. She was taken in by these Potemkin villages and she was well pleased. To increase his sense of well-being in the early 1770s, Potemkin paid 40,000 rubles to Field Marshal Razumovskii for a 50-piece orchestra made up of slave serfs. They were to play continuously around his own palace. The music didn't help. He fell into a deep gloom.

12

Auntie dies – a new upheaval!
Peter is now Tsar Peter the Third!
Catherine, crowned Duchess,
Is at risk on the razor's edge between throne
And dungeon depending on the
Tsar's distemper.
At a blithe court party an intoxicated
Tsar insults Catherine, shouting:
"You are a German fool!"
          And again:
"You are a German fool!"
But she is already in cahoots with the Boyar
Duma, and her courtier friends – Orlov and
Potemkin – are not her only hope.

13

Then the Tsar is arrested and dies.
Whether the thirty-three-year-old Catherine of
Prussia
Is involved in his death is unclear.
September 1762.
At Assumption Cathedral in the heart
Of the Moscow Kremlin
The great upheaval happens!
Wearing
An ermine gown of four thousand skins,
Bejewelled from crown
To toe she is appointed:
"Lady Catherine, Auto-
Crat and Empress of all the Russias!"

ZAHA HADID

VIII

OF DECONSTRUCTION

1

What does "deconstruction" mean?
A question for the witless
Or probably for all of us –
We need to know –
Is it something aggressive?
Dismantled? Demolished? or
Fragile? Breakable?
So simple in my current case –
Deconstruction means that which has, as yet,
No meaning
And that what exists – dismantled
In itself – is waiting for a given meaning
Thus
Deconstruction attempts to undermine the
Oppositional presence of a particular thing
Through a sense of its absence –
A paradoxically mad statement –
We can say bravely that
Rationality is a disengaged
Engagement with
Irrationality
Or, love is a singular kind of hate
Thus

If you don't know the meaning of
Something it is deconstructive or,
Deconstruction is the way something
Unknown becomes known

2

The term "deconstruction" was coined by the French philosopher, Jacques Derrida, in the 1960s as he set out to extend the philosophical excursions of Nietzsche and Heidegger

3

Inane concrete and glass metal pieces
Are deconstructive in themselves
They become a building
After construction!
If an artist wants to freeze ideational
Details in high art
Archived as architecture, for some 20 years
He prays
To DECONSTRUCTION as a philosophy
Consider this – on behalf of the population of Toronto –
ROM, the Royal Ontario Museum, is
Kaleidoscopic sharp–angled cladding
It is absolutely deconstructive
But go inside, look at the non-ornamental
Environment, the
Interiors, the prisms' inner
Ceilings streaming in
Different directions – it is
Deconstructive
Yet the exhibits themselves feel
Constructive and quite comfortable,
Like a gigantic stegosaurus

Gladly spreading its
Thousand vertebrae in non-Euclidian
Curved dynamic spheres

4

Deconstructivism or deconstruction in architecture is a development of postmodern architecture from the late 1980s. It is characterized by ideas of fragmentation, an interest in manipulating ideas of a structure's surface or skin, non-rectilinear shapes which serve to distort and dislocate some of the basic elements of architecture.

5

Return outside: cladding, facades of glass
Shifting pyramids
Dissolve the boring boxes within boxes
Of the Toronto cityscape
The idea of fragmentation
Distorts and dislocates
Into an artistic chaos,
An unpredictability of form
A constructive life of
Deconstructive joy in the eye of
Art
I.e. architecture
Not too long ago – in 1982 – we got
The first Parisian landscape of complex
Buildings – de la Villette, by architect
Bernard Tschumi –
Inspired by the Post-Revolutionary
Russian Constructivist
Kazimir Malevich

6

Built upon the new deconstructivist philosophy
Of Jacques Derrida,
Disciple of Nietzsche and Martin Heidegger
And then   in 1988
A MoMA exhibition
Organized by two American progressive
Architects   Philip Johnson and Mark Wigley
A new label "Deconstruction"
With new architects
Frank Gehry – Zaha Hadid
Peter Eisenman – Daniel Liebeskind
Bernard Tschumi – Rem Koolhaas
An *au courant* construction style of
Many buildings posing Hamlet's
Question – build or not to build?
A metaphysical notion of presence –
Of absence at the same moment –
An assertion of the lasting
Consequences of instability
As it is made stable
A lofty yearning for the Pisan tower's

Longevity of presence
Or, as Philip Johnson says   all architects
Want life beyond their deaths

7   *The Great Iraqi Woman Architect, Zaha Hadid*

> "I have won what? The Pritzker Prize?
> Would you say that a second time?"
> —Mrs. Hadid's phone call

A new Art in time came to the World to say goodbye to the
history of architecture's gravity, to the Pole-Beam
structures under construction, to the column-frieze-architrave! Now
new physical rules chime! Forget gravity! Greet the balance

of dynamic substance! The cosmic fantasy of Art-Designers!
Along with the Art-Diva, the Baghdad-Iraqi-born ZAHA
HADID, an architect who has absorbed Muslim & Western European
Culture, filling it with festive green-blue-glare mosaic mosques!

She came to London in the '70s to conquer the Euclid-Parallels,
The Einstein-Relativity laws, to turn the false gesture of
Post-Modernism toward an abstract and honest Deconstructivism
or Deconstruction, digging through art history's past.

*"I was greatly influenced by early Russian abstract artists,
mainly Malevich & El Lissitsky, applying their theories to my architecture."*

ZAHA, with her childlike character, her genius, became a
non-British Avant-Garde Lady flying into Anti-Gravity,

into her Bird-Beaked Sky-Scale Design, the flooding
parallel-unparallel wall-roof-skin, her adolescent curiosity
in fish-eye-perspective on our dizzy heads!
Oh! Her Zero-Gravity "Paper Architecture." But today

ZAHA – spans our Globe with this long
Line of her REAL Whirl-Symphonies – in Dubai,
in Germany, Japan, US, Italy, Hong Kong! Oh Great Lady!
Ms. Hadid, I open your internet site. You enter my territory!

IX

OF A FOOTPRINT
IN THE HEART

1

the anthill crowd produces loneliness
the real calm
between ants is
the crowd's plain and simple
absence of connection
between birth and death   the call
to live alone in the mind, in a life
habitual to all
where no one needs to wear
the wild look of a desert stranger,
a big beard, tattered clothes
carrying a goatskin umbrella, a
Robinson dressed in
his loneliness, the loneliness
everyone lives through
a philosophical survival, isolated
as all ants
                are separate in the
                crowded
                anthill

a cosmic confluence of souls
ants
        alive and breathing deeply
functional at work
skittering over the land
leaving no footprints

2

"One day, about noon, going towards my boat, I was exceedingly surprised with the print of a man's naked foot on the shore, which was very plain to be seen in the sand." Daniel Defoe and his Mr. Crusoe is a man who overcomes self-pity, and who, after twenty-four agonizing years of solitude, discovers a human footprint in the sand...

3

the dusty road explores millions
of walking feet
from which someone
is needed
just a lone...
or just the lone trace
of one print... one footprint...

one foot
that hints at hope, at the loneliness
that Defoe's Crusoe found in the wet sand,
signal for an ambiguous spiritual future
to live until Friday
and meet Friday
Robinson
surprised seeing the print
of a man's naked foot
(an SOS from Defoe's island soul)
the trembling ocean's pristine shore
friable sand for a footprint
the early morning sea tide having gone out
a crucial moment
400 years ago

though nothing is changed on the desert island
of the anthill
as ants wait and wait for something
for anything
                              an event that will
be a great medieval festival featuring
the shouldering of
a long yellow straw log
ants so obediently close
to each other now

4

       then they dance at play
              listening to jazz
holding a light plastic straw
              to drink with
leaving their natural spirit
      behind a door
           to lie on an asphalt bank
    a sandy shore
indifferent   projecting
a footprint
of itself

5

ants need to pray   it is extremely
                                important
to find a day
                any day a Friday
but not the day Cannibals cook
their meat
such days are perfect
Fridays
especially for man-eaters
                        waiting
        for footprints
traces in the sand
        the wind wipes away
waves wash away
leaving prehistoric fossils
caught between layers of coal
the seizure
        of a butterfly in flight
an absent-minded insect
                        accompanied
by a stegosaurus in dense blind foliage

outside the presumptions of poetry
reality is real prose
washing, after a run of waves,
all prints away
sorrowful footprints embedded in
                            someone's solitary

heart

RICHARD STRAUSS

X

OF MUSIC

Man is a god when he dreams, a beggar when he thinks.
—FRIEDRICH HÖLDERLIN

(overture)

Drums fanfare gongs chimes

Accompany the cosmic craft,
The high-flying hurricane of a mind
Amidst a dark empty void
Overarched by cold twinkling stars

Ringing metal resounds
Tracings of a geometric trajectory,

The long multi-year Space Odyssey
2001 – 1900 – 1800 or – 800 BC
Blind Homer's blessing –

Footloose with his poetic harp

From snow-capped mountains to verdant valleys

Above a dusty earth and storm-tossed waves

(part one)

Singing his authentic tone-poems
Gently strumming internal strings
Melodies reverberate rife with death in life and
In reverse, resurrection, and
Swift winds
Acclimated to

The moon, to the phosphorescent Aegean waves
Of ancient Attica as they engage the dangers
Of a new modern technology

On the edge of the horizon of a

Crimson Zarathustran dawn
Rattling prophetic words rather than
Ancient harmonies – a new inhuman angle to

This post-Nietzschean era –

To the dry thunder of bells cracking –
God being dead – the music continues
As the poet straddles

Modernism, suspicious of fragile ice crystals
Falling from unsettled skies

Incantation of a Volsung Saga's choristers while in flight,
High sonorous voices
Confused, mystified
By the gloom-struck whore of
Black Maidanek and black Mauthausen –

(part two)

Agamemnon's Motif

Composer's arrows shot guilelessly
The only target a Hellenic sky
God Zeus lights up human life and love
E-l-e-c-t-r-a – a girl's fight against enslavement
Against her mother Clytemnestra's treason

Image of the Motherland, two new
Faces of Janus – the second
A male face is a mother's paramour who
Murdered Agamemnon with a knife
And he is not a noble Knight of the Fatherland
He's Electra's enemy – her father's killer
The sound of broken glass echoes the shame
Of these awful muddled circumstances
But then a chord of hope for the future
Zeus again fires up lightning that
Dissolves in the sky, heavy rain clouds –

(part three)

During the 1930s, Richard Strauss allowed himself to accept – without facing up to their full import – the circumstances created in Germany by the Nazis. He conducted at Bayreuth after Toscanini had withdrawn. But he was frustrated at being unable to work with his Jewish librettist, Stefan Zweig. During the war years, when he mainly lived in Vienna, he and the Nazi authorities lived in little more than mutual toleration. When Germany was defeated, and the opera houses destroyed, Strauss wrote an intense lament for Metamorphosen, executed with a grace worthy of his beloved Mozart.

(a last chord)

The bloodied '40s are history's outrider
The joy of the 1900s, when Electra engages
Listeners with her battle sorrows, becomes
The orchestra's solemn thematic
Metaphor for the surviving memory
Of time's martyrs

Metallic ring of a vengeful bell
Chromatic harmony of thunderstorms
The complex chords of staying alive

MARLENE DIETRICH

XI

OF POP

Compassion. Without it you mean little.
—*ABC* by Marlene Dietrich

The heavens are falling down
I can't even breathe.
—MICHAEL JACKSON

1

The anthracitic King
Becomes – not glossy chocolate –
But fades into the insane shine of spider webs
Into a masked pale complexion
And then beneath the green weed
Of his soul's refuge in the land of foliage and
Flowers the King is protected from
The pricks of the white rose,
Becoming Peter Pan in flight through an endlessly
Benevolent childhood

He needs to hold in his white glove a
Dangerous bouquet, his soil, his land

To transform black into a gentle light

And – the white rose's pearl – into ochre beige,
Into the blown blue of a blossom
Beneath the shining
Of a revolutionary chemical reaction

Nature's kaleidoscopic whirl
Wherein he is to be severely sentenced
By a syringe man who shares his insanity

2

The cherubim King as Blue Angel comes
To Paris to ask for a sympathetic song from
A legendary Angel on her last legs – suffering
Blue angst as well
The reclusive cinematic diva
The King's goal is to let her revel in his sadness

He comes carrying his loving
Intelligent pet monkey
And the King is told by the diva's doorman
"I won't talk to the glee monkey"

O the catastrophe of her stern condemnation
"I won't to talk to glee monkey"
Words – heavy stones in his soul
As he wonders where he might find an umbrella
To keep his cloying pet out of the rain,
Sub-angel in hurried disarray

3

"Lili Marlene" is a song based on a German poem from 1915. It became popular in 1938. Marlene Dietrich made this song a favourite for troops of every nation during the Second World War.

LILI MARLENE
(original German version)

Vor der Kaserne,
Vor dem grossen Tor
Stand eine Laterne
Und steht sie noch davor
So woll'n wir uns da wieder she'n
Wie einst Lili Marlene,
Wwie einst Lili Marlene
Unsere beide Schatten
Sah'n wie einer aus
Das wir so lie uns hatten
Das sah man gleich daraus
Und alle Leute soll'n es she'n
Wie einst Lili Marlene,
Wie einst Lili

4

And the King takes not a Paris but a
Cherbourg waterproof umbrella from a
Girl singing in the '60s rain

And the King puts on her angelic mask
As he runs toward the applause of the crowd

And a klieg-lit stage highlights his songs
And the mime's dance
And live tropical green cooling leaves
And the broad brim of his black hat
And Marcel Marceau's white face
And flying moon feet
And the King's soul dancers are hooligans
As they mimic his soft sophisticated strut
But for all their muscled masculinity they cannot
Protect the King
Under his Cherbourg umbrella
From a silver mystery syringe kept inside
A gold empty coffin

XII

OF THE FUTURE

We know little of the things for which we pray.
—GEOFFREY CHAUCER

1

Eureka! he utters a raving verse!
A baby begins to see into the past.
Space hanging from his cradle.
He guesses tomorrow's future.

Poetry is not archeology,
Not an organized search
With a prickly fossil in his
Procrustean bed, he feels the explosive
Clap of a pterodactyl's wings.

He sees bearded Darwin's smirking eyes
The poet also smiles – as he stands before
The abyss of our apish origins
Intuitively projecting the whole of our history.

2

Consciousness that has esoteric
Roots in the subconscious
The encoded unborn technology

Of a baby's cosmic vision

His immortal high-tech thinking,
A human wave-machine
Instead of a bio-brain – still breakable
And vulnerable and unprotected
A bearded god's creation – Neanderthal –
"The poet's eye in a fine frenzy
Rolling" – he sings a
Petrarchan sonnet   a serenade
It's time to alter our archaic inner selves!
Humans sport a bony skeleton

3

Lit by the luminous vibrancy of
Flashing plasma – a man becomes a
Poet – a great human microcosm – with all
Cosmic planets parallel

He might be a signal, syncopated rays whirling
Within the vortex, the pool's spiral dialogue

Poetic incursion into outer space, a reverberation
No revolution! No war! No blood!
Horned Mephistopheles becomes a lover

Of his internal shadow, friend Faust!

4

Futurism came into being with the appearance of a manifesto published by the poet, Filippo Marinetti, on the front page of the February 20, 1909, issue of Le Figaro. *Futurism was presented as a modernist movement celebrating the future technological era. The car, the plane, the industrial town were presented as representing motion in modern life and the technological triumph of man over nature.*

5

Forever young cosmic beam
His phantasmagoric Gretchen
Unburdened by the Devil's Paradise,
Auschwitz – greets
A new art free of night singing beneath windows
Plasma-bio craft machines   a flying soul
Idea of perpetual technology
Sophisticated breathing, thought aflame
God's sonnet song
Plasmic cosmic poetry

DAVID

XIII

OF MICHELANGELO AND VITTORIA COLONNA

1

On the day
I came to Florence
to see the Birth
of Venus by Botticelli
the Gallery was closed

due to terrorism
(were the terrorists cousins once-removed
from those who bombed the Uffizi

back in the '90s?).
Today's political thugs
should know that
David is standing
guard in the Piazza. Staring
sepulchral white, ever young
neo-Platonic nuance chiselled

blindly into the blue abyss
out of solid Carrera marble.

2

Vasari on Michelangelo's David: *"When it was built up, and all was finished, he uncovered it, and it cannot be denied that this work has carried off the palm from all other statues, modern or ancient, Greek or Latin; and it may be said that neither the Marforio at Rome, nor the Tiber and the Nile of the Belvedere, nor the Giants of Monte Cavallo, are equal to it in any respect, with such just proportion, beauty and excellence did Michelangelo finish it."*

3

In 1536, some ten years after
the Grand Constable of Naples,
Ferrante Francesco d'Avalos di Pescara
died from wounds received at the battle of Pavia,
his wife, the Marchesa Vittoria Colonna,
an ascetic beauty, a known sonneteer,
arrived in Rome from Ischia.
She housed herself as one of the *Spiritual Group* –
reformers of the Church –
in a monastery
in Capite with the Sisters of San Silvestro
who believed they possessed the
"preserved head of St. John the Baptist."

Intent on meeting Michelangelo,
she went to him by carriage carrying gifts:
her madrigal to Christ, a breviary,
and perhaps a relic of a saint local to Ischia.
She went to the Sistine Chapel
to talk to the architect Donato Bramante
where she looked up into
an empty vaulted space

looked up and saw
mildew and moss and paint peeling from the walls

where she looked up and – oh! – WHO IS THIS MAN?
so dour and hawk-eyed
is that HIM? – oh!

it happened in 1536!
she a widow of forty-seven
he a sexually bent bachelor over sixty.

4

Death, who breaks the marriage band,
In another, boldly presses
The wedding ring into her hand,
And bares her breast to any man.

5

he opens his eyes wildly,
he finds words
quella donna ch'a Dio mi meneva
he surrounds himself with
drawings   quick sketches
fourteen line sonnets   a madrigal
he sings for her, to her, so that
"she comes often to Rome
to pass the summer with him"
it is a burst of affection he's never shown (just
as he's never known his mother), and so,
'enamoured of her divine spirit,'
he wrote to her:

6

"I desired, lady, before I accepted the things which your ladyship has often expressed the will to give me – I desired to produce something for you with my own hand, in order to be as little as possible unworthy of this kindness. I have now come to recognize that the grace of God is not to be bought, and that to keep it waiting is a grievous sin. Therefore I acknowledge my error, and willingly accept your favors. When I possess them, not indeed because I shall have them in my house, but for that I myself shall dwell in them, the place will seem to encircle me with Paradise. For which felicity I shall remain ever more obliged to your ladyship than I am already, if that is possible."

7   *His Self-Portrait*

who do I see? who's keeping
an eye on me in my own mirror
a crouching sun
behind winged clouds,
occluding clouds
that enclose the sun
in a dark night that becomes
fire as fire becomes
language and alphabet
a song, each song
one of God's
spheres, carousels
wherein
what was pell-mell, tainted,
is now
perfect among the
sainted, the elect. Is this
me, a sculptor, painter, at a loss
in front of a cracked old
canvas?
oh – a blade of light
uncovers age
inching around

the corner of my mouth as
I stubbornly move to force
joy out of the world's creation – and
who is that? David? – my brawny
sensual bone-white Piazza giant

stepping, very much alive,
out of the Old Testament
into the holy chapel of my imagination,
my ceiling –
hmm – smirking:

> "You are absent here –
> You were here before"

8

is Donato Bramante my friend?
NO!
he hardly talks to me
he mostly stands behind me

I feel his
breath on my neck – oh!
he is a builder   he loves construction
he loves to handle stones

it's hard for him to understand
what I go through

reaching
blindly for metamorphosis, for a beating heart
inside a cage of ribs
under a shell! A carapace!

under a crystallizing sphere
some form of stability at the core!
I fight an evolving dying world!
I hunker down in a prehistoric rainforest

I steal through darkness to
hide under a canopy of
huge plane trees – hoping
to find God's beginning in an

apish brain
I hammer and chisel at stone space
so I can penetrate
the Womb while shaking off
marble dust
emptying

breath – giving my own lungs
to a curved mask's mouth
hearing a first sigh – a sigh
confirming that God is free

and so it is that
I rescue many Gods! – they rise up from
the dead – rise up from under
the indifferent WHITE of a

Carrera river bank

9

    still
unknown to Them, until they thrill
in running into each other
she with her sonnets – honing in on his ennui, his pain,
invoking his great name, her obvious delight in
theology and disputation,
hers is an ascetic life, conflicted
by the strife
inherent in Man's Creation

    In an undulating
heaven
of clouds inculcating
a vision
of Holy Mary the
Mother of God,
Vittoria Colonna's
face: and Michelangelo Buanorotti
smiles at her, holds her hand, points to several saints who are
on his walls, his ceiling, all installed
since hearing these lines from one of her
sonnets:

O when the tender breeze and my sweet light
Made beautiful the day and pure and clear...
I sought to rise myself on wings from here
My glory disappeared...

10 *A Sonnet to Vittoria Colonna* by Michelangelo

Blest spirit, who with loving tenderness
   Quickenest my heart so old and near to die,
   Who mid thy joys on me dost bend an eye
   Though many nobler men around thee press!
As thou wert erewhile wont my sight to bless,
   So to console my mind thou now dost fly;
   Hope therefore stills the pangs of memory,
   Which coupled with desire my soul's distress.
So finding in thee grace to plead for me –
   Thy thoughts for me sunk in so sad a case –
   He who now writes, returns you thanks for these –
Lo, it were foul and monstrous usury
   To send thee ugliest paintings in the place
   Of thy fair spirit's living phantasies.

11

this stone I call GIANT – it is now mine!
happiness has happened once in this lifetime
for me – a stonecutter – and I got it!
oh a quarry in Carrara in my Tuscany!

oh my fertile Tuscany!
oh shining stone banks of the Serchio River!
HE – my hidden young
gigantic cherub is inside

in the tight mystery of WHITE!
I have so many drawings, drafts!
I like this one – on rice paper
where I wrote a couple of poetic words:

> *David with a sling, And with a bow I am*
> *Michelangelo – a night column is crushed*!

I have this divine image in my mind
it is so inviting!
I cannot wait to crush my Giant Stone!
it needs to be crushed for all the people's joy!

hey my faithful friend helps!
listen:
my sharp hammer begins to strike –
to awake my future DAVID!

but wait wait wait – oh dear!
I will undress your stone shell
I need to touch your marble skin
your embryo in a cradle womb!

in my head lots of prayers are whirling!
fighting heroes from the Bible
my sculpted thoughts
were born out of poetry

Dante and Petrarch talk to me
Ariosto's Orlando shows me my valorous rout!
did you enjoy poetry? – you – unborn being
if you can hear in your dark white prison

there's lots of strong, crafty fellows around –
my faithful help my friends their assistance!
hey! Francesco, Romeo, Fabricio!
stop dancing around this jailed Orthodox god!

I close my eyes – afraid to see his face!
his features are still
under a veil of uncut stone!
but I hear his breath inside his dark cage!

we need to give him Freedom quickly!
the liberty of Florence!
he is ready to fight for the great Medici!
though his eyes are turned toward everlasting Rome!

oh his marble cloth jacket!
take it off – a clumsy chunk – from a Serchio river bank!
do not be shy – show us your saint's Testamental body!
Fabricio – hey, no pants for the final sculpture!

a Calendar (still the old Julian)
runs runs and runs again!
what is the day today? Friday? March? Six? 1504?
am I thirty? – hey! I AM THIRSTY!

Francesco – pour water from this jug
into the glass to drink, to wash the stone dust
from my rough hands!
Crush the surrounding wood and metal armatures!

hey! run quickly for Red Wine! – not from the
marble banks of my Tuscany – but from sunny Sicily!
hey! – my fellows, my fools – my friends:
David smiles at us – oh no! – sorry! Just ME!

XIV

OF CATHERINE'S VOLGA GUESTS

You philosophers are lucky men. You write on paper and paper is patient. Unfortunate Empress that I am, I write on the susceptible skins of living beings.
—CATHERINE THE GREAT

1

As WWII draws to a close
I am a schoolboy in Kazakhstan
Living with my parents far from the Russian-
German theatre of war, the Eastern Front

I see lots of enemies

We are at War with
Fascist Germans, but the Volga also has
Its Germans
Exiled here by special invitation
In the 18th century at the behest of
Catherine the Great, brought in for their

Agricultural skills to the
Volga valley and now this remnant lives with us,
They are all around! They abound!
Are they not my enemies?
My boyish patriotic logic!
For instance, my schoolmate Nora –
In German she is Eleonora!

She has the enemy's blond braids
Long shapely legs!
A slim flexible body!

Is she not dangerous?

The school bullies hate her pale
Blue-eyed non-Russian face.

2

They hate the young enemy
Her ironed school uniform
They tease her cruelly
They hit her with closed fists
She doesn't cry like Russian girls cry
No tears, just a stillness in her eyes

The sad stare of a young female enemy

Her mother worked in our hospital
As a nurse giving pin-prick
Injections to our settlement
Schoolchildren, injections for our health – Soviet
Girls and boys.
I was confused

Oftentimes I ran into Eleonora's father.
This morning unexpectedly I see him.
I know
He lives in the nearby labour camp
That way, he can visit his loving brood

And now he is loping
Along our shallow Kazakh river bed
A branch of the home river, the Volga.

3

The river's sandy shoreline plashed
Under his feet as he kept pace with Wagner's
Bom-be-dee, as if it were played especially for him
Of course I didn't know *die Nebelungen*
Music by Herr Wagner
As a Russian and as a Youth Pioneer wearing a red tie
I knew only the mellifluous melodies of Tchaikovsky
(*Swan Lake* is not *bom-bom-boom* music)
Listened to on our own squeaky gramophone.
But I definitely felt the need in
Nora's father as he kept lockstep with our enemy's
Music-to-run-by on this sporty morning.
Sport? a morning run is not the fashion here
Not in our settlement, and Eleonora's father
(With a sweet polite smile on his sweaty face)
Looks at my surprised boy's face
And he smiles at me – too friendly?

Why is Nora's father running in the morning?
From the Red Army? Why is he so casual?
By now the Front is inside Germany
(Sorry he is a Volga German, but he is German)
Why does he smile? At Catherine the Second's command?

She'd died. She's dead. I'd learnt that.
Otherwise she'd be here with her compatriots,
These enemies,
Hiding in our settlement –
With my smarty-pants little self
In tow, I take off for school...

In 1763, Catherine the Great issued a persuasive Manifesto invifing foreigners to settle in Russia. Because of impoverished conditions in Europe – due to the Seven Years War – and an aggressive campaign by immigration agents, many Germans answered the call to "paradise." During the years from 1764 to 1767, Germans colonized 104 villages in the desolate Volga Valley of Russia near the city of Saratov. Of these, 44 were on the West side, the hilly side (Bergseite) of the Volga River, and 60 villages were on the East side, the meadow side (Wiesenseite). The villages ranged in population from 225 to 250 people each. The emigrants numbered a total of more than seven thousand families, an estimated 25 thousand people. The majority came from Hesse, with southwest Germany being well represented, and fewer coming from other countries. Separate religious affiliations were of primary importance and interdenominational villages were extremely rare. With few exceptions, all of the villages were Lutheran, Reformed or Catholic, and later, Mennonite.

4   *In Memory of Heinrich Petrovich*

the blizzard is a dervish whirl of snow,
and though, with classes ended,
I should go home,
I hold my teacher's hand

my German teacher,
Comrade Heinrich Petrovich
from the outlying Russian-German
Volga district

exiled during WWII
(like my family before the War)
to this arid Asian plot on the planet,
he is of the generation of

Catherine the Great's
agronomist-guests,
and now here he is with me in a
whirling blizzard

my eyes sealed shut by
snow and sleet
my teacher's snow moustache
widens with his smile:

"You are *ein Knabe* snowman,
Advent before Christmas!"
his voice scuttled by
the swell of the storm.

"This is Christmas, for real!
This godless atheistic cold front, this
Russia of Kazakhstan!
Where there is
Brutal war! Where the Nazis are!"

XV

OF FIDEL CASTRO

I fixed an eye on Fidel twice. Once – ALIVE :
As a student – it was in Moscow – loping through Theatre
Square to the subway after my lectures.

Decades ago!

Passing the Bolshoi, elbowed by the strolling
Muscovites who'd transformed themselves into a huge
Rambunctious crowd. I was infected by curiosity!

What did I see? Oh!

A ghost. HE   FIDEL   moved   not walked   DANCED!
Passionately, smiling broadly, approaching the Kremlin.

Soviet admirers exulting:

VIVA CUBA! VIVA CUBA! VIVA CUBA!
Stunned   I watched him ascend the Bolshoi's porch!

Just a couple of days ago, here,
On this same stage, I'd enjoyed the grand Cuban ballerina
Alicia Alonso! How come she was not dancing with him?
Two masters of the pirouette?

I leaned against a column, afraid of the
Herd of enthusiastic demonstrators!

So happy to see this legend among revolutionaries,
Faithful friend of our USSR – actually DANCE!

I cried : Hurray!

And than the second time
I happened to see HIM recently! Only he was much younger!

How? Where?

I spent a night with a TCM tv program on my
Toshiba – a show about him. My Fidel – as a teenage hoofer
At a Havana ambassadorial Ball in 1946.

He'd been invited to the US Embassy, a young
Good-looking dancer, for a movie shoot – *Holiday in Mexico*!

"The first and last time he was invited to meet the
US Ambassador"! A pity – such a huge loss to art:

Because of his Communist ambitions we – all of us –
Lost a man up on his toes, a Ballet Star!

An adornment at all solemn social gatherings
At the White House! Clearly, he loved the US Presidency
As a young man – you can read Fidel's teenage letter –

The spelling is his :

November 6, 1940

Mr Franklin Roosvelt, President of the United States.

*My good friend Roosvelt I don't know very English,
but I know as much as write to you. I like to hear the radio,
and I am very happy, because I heard in it, that you will be
President for a new (periodo).*

*If you like, give me a ten dollars bill green American, in
the letter, because never, I have not seen a ten dollars bill
green American and I would like to have one of them.
(Thank you very much)*

Good by. Your friend, Fidel Castro

If you want iron to make your ships I will show to you the bigest (minas) of iron of the land. They are in Mayari Oriente Cuba.

ZARA ZASULICH

XVI

OF TERRORISM

Vera Zasulich – the first terrorist, a Russian woman

Heavy metal chains clang –
Vera Ivanovna! Why did you hate this noble man?
          – Her silence

Petersburg's courtyard of
Lean, occluded windows
Her revolver belted
As she leans against cold stone walls
Cowled in a black shawl
Waiting for Governor Trepov
Vera Ivanovna! Why did you shoot at him?
          – Her silence

1876. The World's first woman
Terrorist, Vera Zasulich enters history
Vera Ivanovna! But why did you try to kill him?
          – Her silence

The middle of the 19th century
"What's to be Done?" – this new common call to the
Russian people – out to change the world
The European climate is so tempting to our intellectuals
1861 – Serfdom is finished in Euro-Slavic Russia

Though such slavery in another guise persists
Vera Ivanovna! Why did you shoot at a governor?
      – Her silence

Why did you shoot? Why did you become
The first woman terrorist? An idea? Stone cold hatred?
Searching for a Way? The Way? Why? Vera Ivanovna!
      – Her silence

Even so, a formal Tsarist trial set this rebellious woman free!
She turned to Karl Marx and
As a now fervent Marxist she asked him
To apply revolutionary theory, independent, of course, of Lenin,
To the Russian Nation – boyars, kulaks, the whole kit-and-kaboodle
      – Her half-silence

Zasulich's lone shot has not been forgotten by the world.
It careened through a long line of revolutionaries. Terrorists.
Yes, the Revolution's victims are sealed like flies
In the amber of what has been done: 9/11 has roots.
      – Our silence

Vladimir Azarov is an architect and poet,
formerly from Moscow, who lives in Toronto.
He has published *Sochi Delirium, Seven Lives, Broken Pastries,*
Mongolian Études, Night Out, Dinner With Catherine the Great,
Strong Words: Pushkin, Akhmatova, Voznesensky in
a Russian and English edition (co-translator Barry Callaghan)
with Exile Editions, and previously:
Imitation, Of Life and Other Small Sacrifices,
The Kiss from Mary Pickford: Cinematic Poems,
and *Voices in Dialogue: Dramatic Poems.*

The interior portraits are by Nina Bunjevac
who is a Toronto-based artist and illustrator.
Her most recent work is the acclaimed graphic novel, *Fatherland*.
www.ninabunjevac.com

Acknowledgements

I am very thankful for the many discussions about writing I have had recently, and over the years of my becoming a poet, with Jay MillAr, Allan Briesmaster, Beatriz Hausner, Ewan Whyte, Bruce Meyer, Allen Sutterfield, Maureen Hynes, Angela Zito, Bill Knock and Jon Apgar.

My gratitude to Barry Callaghan who helped me organize and edit the eclectic nature of these poems. My appreciation to graphic artist Nina Bunjevac for her nine imaginative portrayals of some of the poem's characters. Sincere thanks to Michael Callaghan for his editorial and artistic acumen through the publishing process, and for the support Exile Editions offers to all poets.

In 1962, lying on a Sochi beach, I opened a newspaper and there I saw the big story: MARILYN MONROE DEAD!

This was also the time of the Khrushchev Thaw in Soviet life, and I had chanced to see Billy Wilder's great film, *Some Like It Hot*, featuring that unbelievable beauty, that force of nature, Marilyn Monroe. There on the beach she did not die for me; she settled into my heart. Sochi became, in my memory, not a town but a bell tolling my bond with her.

In 2014, while watching the winter Olympics on television, I came down with a severe flu and a week-long fever that often peaked at 103. She came to me again. My Sochi Beatrice, guiding me through decades of memories: this book is my Sochi delirium.

Vladimir Azarov grew up and came to maturity during a time in the Soviet Union when penal camps and the secret police were ubiquitous. The one great truth that he learned in his own exile, and the world learned from all the great Russian writers, is that almost everything can be taken from an individual but his or her story, his or her undying and unyielding sense of self. Azarov, in his own plain-spoken voice, has composed seven stories about seven lives that are marvellously moving in their seeming simplicity, their actual depth. *Seven Lives* is Vladimir Azarov's childhood experiences of Soviet life transformed into a poetic witnessing.

Few moments, certainly few speeches, in the 20th century so radically altered the flow of international events and specifically the direction of Russian history as Nikita Khrushchev's 1956 attack on the cult of Joseph Stalin. Overnight, a society under the lock and key of ideology and the eye of a secret police was sprung loose, entering into a period that has since come to be known as The Thaw. Azarov has written 26 monologues, each devoted to recollecting sunburst moments of freedom, moments of awareness when millions of people were suddenly coming in from the great cold of Stalin's years of terror.

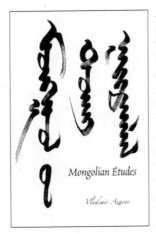

A book made up of letters, poems, and prose pieces that together create a wonderful and idiosyncratic look at Soviet life as witnessed from the edge of that totalitarian empire. Vladimir Azarov was overseeing the design and construction of an Embassy building in the isolated Soviet republic of Mongolia. It was there that he met a remarkable Mongolian woman, and it was through her that he was introduced to the Leningrad world of the great Russian poet, Anna Akhmatova, and her social scientist son, Lev Gumilov. Out of this nostalgic quest emerges, through a newly discovered memoir, a totally unexpected love story involving the Mongolian woman and Gumilov. This enthralling account is a cultural study of the times, a testimony to the endurance of memory and feeling, and a touching exploration of the human condition.

Night Out is Vladimir Azarov's tribute to the architects and visionaries who have had a hand in shaping his inner landscape. From Van Gogh and Gauguin's tempestuous relationship in Arles to the dichotomies of modern-day Tokyo where the bustle of a giant metropolis is set against the Zen calm of monks and cathedral builders, *Night Out* is a celebration of what holds the world together. Vladimir Azarov is by trade an architect, but by nature a poet, and his poetry celebrates the spirit that resides at the core of great artifice.

—Bruce Meyer, Poet Laureate of Barrie, Ontario

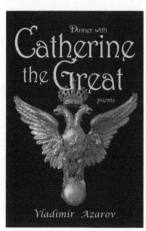

Providing a rare and creative sense of authority's various faces, this collection of poems by Russian architect and Canadian poet Vladimir Azarov travels from intellectual and artistic power to philosophical, military, and imperial power; and above all, personal influence. The verse introduces the persuasiveness, complexities, and intrigues of "table talk" – a European tradition of informed and enlightened conversation that has virtually disappeared from the experience of North American culture. Commanding and informed in their own sense of purpose, these pieces evince a gentle curiosity for greatness, creating an engaging portrait of simple humanity, powerful minds, and memorable ideas.

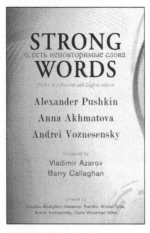

STRONG
о, есть неповторимые слова
WORDS

Poetry in a Russian and English edition

Alexander Pushkin
Anna Akhmatova
Andrei Voznesensky

translated by
Vladimir Azarov
Barry Callaghan

artwork by
Amedeo Modigliani, Alexander Pushkin, Nikolai Tyrsa,
Andrei Voznesensky, Claire Weissman Wilks

This collection of writing presents new translations of a combined 44 poems, alongside the Russian texts. Alexander Pushkin is the greatest of Russian poets, and certainly he is the founder of modern Russian literature. Anna Akhmatova is Russia's singular woman poet and the greatest in Western Culture. Andrei Voznesensky was considered "one of the most daring writers of the Soviet era" and before his death he was both critically and popularly proclaimed "a living classic." These three master poets are brought together through superb translations that engage in their many complexities.

"*Strong Words* achieves something exceptional. This small, powerful selection of poems by Pushkin, Akhmatova and Voznesensky – three distinct poetic voices – creates a mysterious wholeness; one can almost imagine the book as a single poem, so alert are these translations to the elusive narrative of deeply felt human experience. This is what the best poetry is capable of: an entire life illumined in a line or two."

—Anne Michaels, Toronto's Poet Laureate

All of these books by Vladimir Azarov can be ordered direct from the publisher at: www.ExileEditions.com